FAMILIES of Fame & Fortune

THE CURRYS

by Kristin J. Russo

FAST READS

full tilt PRESS

For Lauren, who loved people of all walks of life, and relished hearing their stories.

The Currys
Families of Fame and Fortune

Full Tilt Press
42964 Osgood Road
Fremont, CA 94539
readfulltilt.com

Full Tilt Press publications may be purchased for educational, business, or sales promotional use.

Editorial Credits
Design and layout by Sara Radka
Edited by Renae Gilles
Copyedited by Nikki Ramsay

Image Credits
Getty Images: Allsport/Doug Pensinger, 21 (bottom), Allsport/Ezra Shaw, 26 (top left), Chris Graythen, 3 (bottom), 12 (bottom), Dave Mangels, 3 (top), 15, Ezra Shaw, 7, 17 (bottom), 24, 26 (bottom), 27 (bottom), 28 (left), Facebook/Kelly Sullivan, 3 (middle), 13 (left), 17 (top), GBK Productions/Jerod Harris, cover (left), Jonathan Ferrey, 8, 19, Lachlan Cunningham, 20, Madame Tussauds San Francisco/Beck Diefenbach, 23, NYCWFF/Gustavo Caballero, 27 (top right), Ronald Martinez, 21 (top), 25 (top), 28 (right), Streeter Lecka, 5, 16, 27 (top left), Tequila Avion/Cassidy Sparrow, 9, 13 (top), cover (right), Tom Pennington, 13 (right); Newscom: Icon SMI/Ric Tapia, 10, WENN/FayesVision/FS2, 26 (top right); Pixabay: 27707, background, GDJ, 12 (background); Shutterstock: Nelli Syrotynska, 25 (bottom), Oleksii Sidorov, cover (background); Wikimedia: Iam_chihang, 12 (top)

ISBN: 978-1-62920-846-6 (library binding)
ISBN: 978-1-62920-858-9 (ePub)

Contents

Introduction

Fans packed the Spectrum Center in Charlotte, North Carolina, on February 15, 2019. It was the 68th National Basketball Association (NBA) **All-Star** Weekend. NBA players and fans gathered to celebrate.

All eyes were on Sonya Curry. She was on the half-court line. Bending her knees, she prepared to shoot. With all her might, she launched the ball.

The crowd roared! Sonya's underhanded shot swished through the net. The shot was special. It was dubbed "the official kickoff" of the All-Star celebration. Sonya's husband joined her on the court. Dell Curry is a former NBA superstar. The couple took part in a shooting competition. The event was for **charity**. They faced son Stephen (pronounced "Steffen") and his wife, Ayesha. Stephen's younger brother, Seth, also joined in the fun. He played with his wife, Callie. Sonya's daughter, Sydel, competed too. So did Sydel's husband, NBA guard Damion Lee.

The Curry family wowed the crowd. They showed the world why they are called "Basketball's First Family."

All-Star: an outstanding sports player

charity: an organization that provides help and money for people in need

After the family shootout, Stephen played in the 2019 All-Star Game.

Chapter 1

MEET THE CURRYS

The Curry family loves to have fun together. They also take the game of basketball very seriously. Stephen and Seth faced off against each other in the NBA 2019 Western Conference Finals. Stephen played for the Golden State Warriors. Seth played for the Portland Trail Blazers. The competition was tense.

It was the first time in NBA history that brothers played against one another in a conference final. Their parents flipped a coin. This decided which jersey they would wear in support of their sons. Dell wore a Warrior jersey. Sonya dressed in Trail Blazer colors.

"We're not rooting for either one wholeheartedly," Dell told a reporter at the event. "We're rooting for both to play well, but you can't root for one team over the other."

ambidextrous: able to use the right and left hands equally well

Stephen said he had mixed feelings about guarding Seth in 2019. At times, he wanted his brother to score.

Famous Fact

While preferring his right hand, Dell Curry is known to be **ambidextrous.** Stephen Curry shares this trait.

Seth said the 2019 match-up was "a special time for both of us and something we'll always remember."

Stephen and Seth both took shot after shot in the match-up. In the end, Stephen's team won the title. Though winning meant his younger brother's team had to lose, Stephen said facing Seth on the court was an unforgettable experience. "We'll remember this for the rest of our lives," he said.

It's no surprise that Stephen, Seth, and their sister Sydel love sports. They were raised by parents who enjoy competition. Sonya was a star athlete in high school. She played volleyball at Virginia Tech. There, she met her future husband, Dell Curry.

Dell played high school baseball and basketball. He was a starter for the Virginia Tech Hokies. He was named Player of the Year in 1986. That same year, he was **drafted** into the NBA. Dell and Sonya married in 1988. They raised their young family while traveling with Dell's teams. The boys decided they wanted to follow their father into the NBA. Like her mother, Sydel shined as a volleyball player in high school and college.

draft: when a professional sports team chooses a player from high school or college

stature: someone's height

Sonya and Dell Curry

SONYA CURRY

Sonya Curry is 5 feet, 3 inches (1.6 meters) tall. Her short **stature** did not hold her back from success in sports. She won a state basketball championship in high school. In college, she made 57 aces. An ace is a type of volleyball serve. It lands in the opponents' court before a player can reach it. This feat earned her a school record. Sonya has the sixth-most aces in a single season as a junior.

Chapter 2

CURRY FAMILY HISTORY

Education was just as important as sports to the Curry kids. The children attended a **Montessori** school through grade six. Sonya started the school in Huntersville, North Carolina. For middle and high school, they went to small Christian schools.

Stephen became Davidson College's all-time leading scorer in 2009.

As young boys, Stephen and Seth loved to go to warm-up practices with Dell. They shot baskets and ran around the court. The boys became friends with their dad's teammates, famous NBA players.

Stephen wanted to go to college at his parents' **alma mater**, Virginia Tech. But he was not **recruited** to play on the team. Instead, he attended Davidson College in North Carolina. In 2009, the young man was drafted by the Golden State Warriors. He was the seventh overall pick. Despite a rocky start to his career, Stephen would become a record-breaking player.

Seth also struggled to find his place. He went to Duke University. There, he was a top scorer. But he was not selected by any team in the 2013 draft. The Golden State Warriors signed him on to play that summer. But Seth was let go after a few **exhibition games**. The young player was traded nearly every year. He was on seven more teams before being traded to the Philadelphia 76ers in November 2020. Although he missed some games in the 2020–21 season due to injuries, Seth has scored in nearly every game he has played for the 76ers. As of April 2021, Seth averaged 12.6 points per game.

· ·

Montessori: an education system for children that develops interests naturally, rather than using formal teaching methods

alma mater: the school, college, or university that someone attended in the past

recruit: when someone from a college invites a high school athlete to join their team

exhibition game: a game that doesn't count toward a team's or players' rankings or official scores

Sydel excelled in volleyball and basketball. In high school, she had to choose one. Like her mother, Sydel chose volleyball. She helped her team win big. They broke the record for most wins in a season in 2012.

Sydel went on to North Carolina's Elon University. A knee injury **sidelined** the athlete in her first year. But she didn't stay down long.

Curry Family Tree

Dell Curry
June 25, 1964
former NBA player, sports commentator

Stephen Curry
March 14, 1988
NBA player

Ayesha Disa Curry
March 23, 1989
TV personality, cook, and author

Riley Elizabeth
July 19, 2012

Ryan Carson
July 10, 2015

Canon Wardell Jack
July 2, 2018

Sydel said, "The best advice from my family is that it's okay to mess up . . . Always take what has happened and learn from it, good or bad, and become a better person." In her junior year, she led the league with 1,170 total **assists** and 10.35 assists per set.

· ·

sideline: to stop someone from playing or participating

assist: in sports, an action that helps a teammate to score

Sonya (Adams) Curry

May 30, 1966

educator

Callie Rivers Curry	**Seth Curry**	**Sydel Curry**	**Damion Lee**
September 17, 1989	*August 23, 1990*	*October 20, 1994*	*October 21, 1992*
volleyball player	NBA player	volleyball player and entrepreneur	NBA player

Carter "CeCe" Lynn

May 9, 2018

Chapter 3

SUPER STARDOM

Stephen has natural talent. But he also puts in practice time. Stephen makes 300 to 500 shots a day. "You've got to be able to put in the time and the work. That's how I got here. That's how I continue to get better every single day," he said.

The hard work paid off with his 2015–16 season. Stephen sank 402 3-pointers. The Warriors won a record 73 games. Stephen was named MVP. It was by **unanimous** vote. Stephen became an NBA superstar. And he did it by playing in a new way. Dunking used to be the goal. But Stephen showed shooting skills can take a player to the top too.

Stephen is not the only star in his household. His wife Ayesha is a famous cook. She started out as an actress. Then her passion for cooking took over. She wrote a cookbook in 2016. It is called *The Seasoned Life*. Ayesha has been on several cooking shows. She runs restaurants and even has her own cookware business.

At home, Ayesha cooks family meals. She creates a balanced diet of healthy food. This keeps Stephen playing his best. Ayesha also loves to cook with her kids. "It's messy. But the memories you make are worth it," she said.

unanimous: agreed to by every member of a group

Stephen Curry and Ayesha attended the Nickelodeon Kids' Choice Sports Awards in 2016.

Famous Fact

Stephen and his daughter Riley have a secret handshake. It starts with a high five and ends with a kiss.

Seth started in 86 games during his 3 seasons with Duke University.

Seth was a star player for Duke University. He was a regular in the starting lineup. In the 2011–12 season, he earned the team's second-highest average. But he had a rocky start in the NBA. He was hired and let go from several teams. Between 2016 and 2020, he played for the Dallas Mavericks and the Portland Trail Blazers. Then in 2020, he signed a contract with the Philadelphia 76ers. The player is still looking for the right fit in the NBA.

Like the Currys, Callie Rivers grew up in the NBA. Her father is Glen Anton "Doc" Rivers. He played in the NBA in the 1980s. Doc is now head coach of the Philadelphia 76ers. Callie's three brothers are also basketball players. Callie and Seth met when they were young. They joined the two basketball families with their marriage in 2019. Seth had proposed on Valentine's Day that year. It was during the All-Star Weekend.

Sydel stopped playing volleyball in 2017. She now focuses on her work. She is a **social media influencer**. Sydel has a YouTube channel. She also writes a blog. Her Instagram account has hundreds of thousands of followers. Sydel shares her passion for fitness, fashion, and charity work. Sydel is still involved in sports. Her husband, Damion Lee, is a rising star in the NBA.

Sydel and Sonya have always enjoyed a close relationship. In 2019, Sydel called Sonya "the best mother in the world."

A BAD SCOUTING REPORT

In 2009, a scout was looking at college players for the NBA draft. He wrote a report on Stephen Curry. The scout was not impressed by the young player. He noted that Stephen would have to work very hard to make it in the NBA. His report said that Stephen was "far below NBA standard in regard to explosiveness and athleticism." Stephen went on to become an NBA champion and Most Valuable Player (MVP). He worked hard to prove that he did have the drive and talent to make it in the NBA.

social media influencer: a user with many followers who trust their advice and recommendations for products

Chapter 4

CURRY FAMILY VALUES

Stephen and Ayesha balance their careers with family. Stephen spends as much time as he can with his kids. He has tea parties with his daughters. Everyone sits down for home-cooked meals together. Stephen's kids are part of his career too. His daughter often joins him at press conferences.

Seth and Callie had a daughter of their own in 2018. The family hopes that the new generation plays sports too. Doc Rivers said he hopes their kids have the "Curry shot and the Rivers athleticism."

Stephen and Seth are raising their kids in famous families. They are trying to shelter them from too much fame. Seth and Callie keep their daughter out of the media. Stephen and Ayesha want to keep their kids humble too. They are giving them "a normal life in terms of treating people the right way, having respect, not getting too big-headed, and feeling like everything's about them," Stephen said.

Famous Fact

The Curry family values honesty. In college, Stephen found a wallet. There was $160 inside. The young man found the owner and returned it.

Stephen appreciates having his father close to his career. "I never take it for granted, the fact that I'm able to play basketball at this level and have my dad still a part of the league."

The Currys live all across the country, from California to North Carolina. They still find ways to connect. The family celebrates any chance for a "mini family reunion." The 2019 All-Star Weekend was one such event.

The whole gang gets together for sunny family vacations. In 2016, they went to Hawaii. The next year, they visited Turks and Caicos. Those are islands in the Bahamas. The family enjoys each other's company. They spend time at the beach and play card games. Uno is a family favorite.

Technology helps when people can't be there in person. In 2020, the family wasn't able to travel. They kept in touch by using computers instead. Dell said he video chatted with his children and grandchildren every day.

Ayesha was grand marshal for the GoPro Grand Prix of Sonoma in 2016. She and Stephen got to meet racing legend Mario Andretti.

The Curry family also believes it's important to give back to their fans. Dell and Sonya started the Dell Curry Foundation in 1998. The organization helps young people with school, jobs, and health issues.

Dell and Sonya's **philanthropy** has inspired their children. In 2019, Stephen and Ayesha launched the Eat. Learn. Play. Foundation. It helps young people in Oakland, California. In 2020, the foundation donated a million meals. The food helped kids whose schools had closed down during the pandemic.

Riley and Ryan are growing up around the NBA, just like Stephen and Seth did.

COMPARING FATHER AND SON

Sports **analysts** like to compare Dell and his son Stephen's 3-pointer skills. Both have impressive records. Dell has a career total of 1,245 3-pointers. But Stephen holds the record for making the most 3-point shots in a single season. This means Stephen made a third of his father's total career record shots in only one season. He made 402 in the 2015–16 season. Dell retired from the NBA in 2002, but Stephen has many more years to shoot 3-pointers.

philanthropy: giving money to help improve other people's lives

analyst: someone who studies something closely and carefully

Chapter 5

A LOOK AHEAD

Each member of the Curry family is growing their careers. Dell played for 10 years with the Charlotte Hornets. Now he is a commentator for the team. He works on television broadcasts of their games.

Sonya is president of the school that she started when her kids were young. As a member of the NBA's royal family, she takes part in many media events. This includes interviews and panel discussions. She talks about tough issues, such as racism.

In 2020, Ayesha took the next step in her career. She launched a magazine. Ayesha shares her thoughts on food, family, and keeping a home. As a woman of color, she made a magazine that reflects real people. It "celebrates diversity and **inclusivity**," she said.

With his wife's support, Stephen is branching out into media. He cofounded a production company in 2019. It is called Unanimous Media. The company makes movies and TV shows. Stephen said his goal is "to inspire and move people."

Famous Fact

Ayesha and Stephen met when they were 14 and 15 years old. Their first date was to Madame Tussauds in Hollywood as teenagers.

inclusivity: including people who might otherwise be left out, such as minorities or people with disabilities

Stephen's family enjoyed the unveiling of his wax figure at the Madame Tussauds wax museum in San Francisco.

Sonya travels to games and supports her growing family on and off the court. She also continues to work as a school administrator. She runs the Montessori School that she started.

Sydel is growing her presence on social media. Sydel and Damion have a YouTube channel. They share videos about staying active and healthy. Sydel hosted a show on Facebook Watch. It was called "Sydel Takes On." She interviewed the siblings of famous people. Sydel shared her own stories as a member of a famous family.

In 2020, Damion signed a new contract. He and Stephen are now Warriors teammates. For years, Damion played at a lower level of basketball. Joining the Warriors is a huge opportunity.

Damion thanked his brother-in-law Seth for inspiring him to stick with it. "Seth is one of the biggest inspirations in my life, just knowing everything he's been through. And knowing how he's worked so hard to make a name for himself and continues to make a name for himself," he said.

Despite strong shooting from Damion Lee, the Warriors fell to the San Antonio Spurs on November 1, 2019.

With Seth now playing for the Philadelphia 76ers, he may face brother Stephen on the court once more. Stephen began his 12th season with the Golden State Warriors in 2020. He will no doubt try to break his own stellar shooting records. He may even go for a third MVP trophy. Both brothers are sure to add to the exciting Curry basketball legacy.

Seth played for the Dallas Mavericks before getting traded to the Philadelphia 76ers.

STEPHEN'S FAVORITE RECIPE

Sometimes Stephen helps out by cooking dinner. He usually cooks a simple pasta dish.

Ingredients

12 oz. egg noodles
8 oz. chopped pancetta (or bacon)
2 red bell peppers, seeded and diced
1 cup finely grated Parmesan
handful of fresh basil leaves

Step 1. Cook noodles according to the package. Drain noodles. Save ½ cup of pasta water. Return noodles to pot.

Step 2. Cook pancetta or bacon until crisp. Remove from pan, leaving about ¼ cup of fat. Add peppers to pan and cook until soft.

Step 3. Add the pancetta, peppers, Parmesan, and half of the pasta water to the noodles. Stir. Add more pasta water if the mixture is dry. Mix in basil and serve!

2010

Callie Rivers graduates from Florida University. While there, she is a star member of the Gators volleyball team.

2002

Dell retires from the NBA.

2009

Stephen is drafted by the NBA on June 25, his father's birthday. He is a first-round pick for the Golden State Warriors.

2014

Seth is named All-Star in the NBA's D-League.

2021

Stephen and Seth face off in a match-up between the Warriors and the 76ers. The game is tied 55-55 after the first half. Stephen's Warriors pull ahead and win 107-96.

2015

Stephen wins his first MVP Award. He earns his second the next year.

2017

Sydel graduates from Elon University with a degree in psychology.

Quiz

1. What college did both Dell and Sonya attend?

2. What NBA team did Dell play on for 10 years?

3. What type of school did Sonya Curry establish?

4. What sport did both Sonya and Sydel play in college?

5. What is the name of Ayesha's cookbook?

6. Whose team won the 2021 match-up?

7. What is Stephen's goal for his production company?

8. Which family member joined the Warriors in 2020?

Activity

The Currys enjoy competing in many different sports, especially basketball. Exercise helps build healthy bodies. Belonging to a team builds friendships and leadership skills. Research and consider joining an organized sports team.

MATERIALS

- pen and pencil
- local newspaper
- internet access
- helpful adult

STEPS

1. Make a list of your physical skills. Can you run fast? Can you throw with accuracy? Do you have a particular interest, such as swimming or gymnastics?

2. With the help of a teacher, librarian, or trusted adult, look online to find groups or events that host sporting events near you. Does your school have a team? Is there a gym where you can take gymnastics lessons? Is there a recreation league looking for soccer players?

3. Find out when and where the lessons or games take place. Go and watch a session to see if the sport is really something you'd like to do.

4. Make a list of items you will need to compete. Will you need special shoes or other special equipment? Make sure the equipment you use fits properly and is in good repair.

5. With a parent or guardian's permission, fill out your registration form and join! Enjoy making new friends and learning new skills.

Glossary

All-Star: an outstanding sports player

alma mater: the school, college, or university that someone attended in the past

ambidextrous: able to use the right and left hands equally well

analyst: someone who studies something closely and carefully

assist: in sports, an action that helps a teammate to score

charity: an organization that provides help and money for people in need

draft: when a professional sports team chooses a player from high school or college

exhibition game: a game that doesn't count toward a team's or players' rankings or official scores

inclusivity: including people who might otherwise be left out, such as minorities or people with disabilities

Montessori: an education system for children that develops interests naturally, rather than using formal teaching methods

philanthropy: giving money to help improve other people's lives

recruit: when someone from a college invites a high school athlete to join their team

sideline: to stop someone from playing or participating

social media influencer: a user with many followers who trust their advice and recommendations for products

stature: someone's height

unanimous: agreed to by every member of a group

Read More

Ignotofsky, Rachel. *Women in Sports: 50 Fearless Athletes Who Played to Win.* New York: Ten Speed Press, 2017.

Omoth, Tyler Dean. *The NBA Finals.* North Mankato, MN: Capstone Press, 2020.

Silverstein, Natalie. *Simple Acts: The Busy Family's Guide to Giving Back.* Lewisville, NC: Gryphon House. 2019.

Wetzel, Dan. *Epic Athletes: Stephen Curry.* New York: Henry Holt & Co., 2019.

Internet Sites

How to Play Basketball
Watch a basketball instructional video featuring Stephen Curry and other basketball greats.
https://www.youtube.com/watch?v=K9NCz43Ryw4

Sports Illustrated Kids
Read articles on the world of sports, written by kid reporters.
https://www.sikids.com

Women in Sports
Read amazing facts about women in sports.
https://www.factmonster.com/sports/women-sports

Index